Candy Bomber

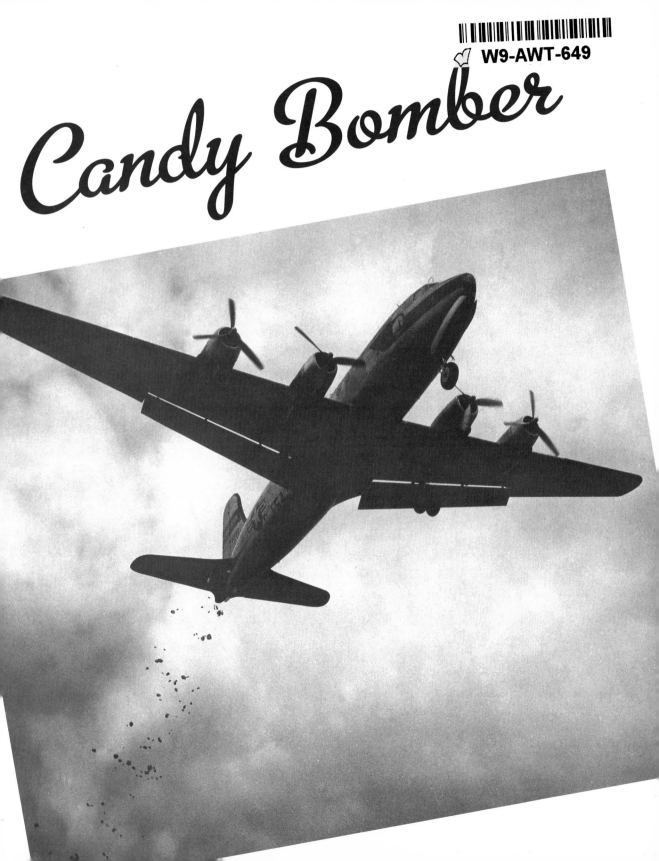

Candy Bomber

The Story of
the Berlin Airlift's
"Chocolate Pilot"

Michael O. Tunnell

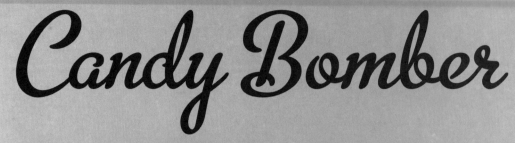

Charlesbridge

To Gail
—M. O. T.

Published by Charlesbridge
85 Main Street
Watertown, MA 02472
(617) 926-0329
www.charlesbridge.com

Library of Congress Cataloging-in-Publication Data
Tunnell, Michael O.
    Candy bomber : the story of the Berlin Airlift's "Chocolate Pilot" /
Michael O. Tunnell.
        p. cm.
    ISBN 978-1-58089-336-7 (reinforced for library use)
    ISBN 978-1-58089-337-4 (softcover)
1. Berlin (Germany)—History—Blockade, 1948–1949—Juvenile literature.
2. Halvorsen, Gail S.—Juvenile literature. 3. United States. Air Force.
Military Airlift Command—Biography—Juvenile literature. 4. Air pilots,
Military—United States—Biography—Juvenile literature. I. Title.
DD881.T845 2010
943'.1550874—dc22 [B]   2009026648

Printed in China
(hc) 10 9 8 7 6 5 4
(sc) 10 9 8 7 6 5

Display type and text type set in MetroScript and Adobe Caslon
Color separations by Jade Productions
Printed and bound April 2013 by Jade Productions in ShenZhen, Guangdong, China
Production supervision by Brian G. Walker
Designed by Diane M. Earley

Half title: Candy parachutes scatter from a Douglas C-54 Skymaster.
Title page: German children wait on the rubble of war, hoping to spot candy-laden parachutes drifting in the wind.

Table of Contents

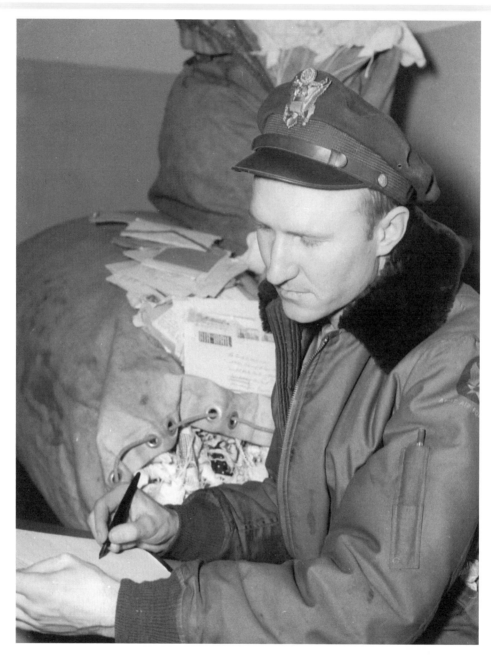

Lt. Gail Halvorsen, a young pilot during the Berlin Airlift (1948–49), answers letters sent to him by children from West Berlin.

Prologue

*W*hen I was a boy I would watch beautiful silver airplanes fly high in the sky, going to faraway places with strange-sounding names. I didn't know then that when I grew up I would fly one of those silver birds myself. I never imagined I would fly food to boys and girls so they would not starve.

This book is special to me because it tells about the people of Berlin who valued freedom over food. The Russians promised them food if they agreed to live under Soviet rule, but they refused. They wanted to be free, even if that meant going hungry. Children felt this way, too. "I can live on thin rations but not without hope," one

Lt. Halvorsen mingles with a friendly crowd at Tempelhof Central Airport.

ten-year-old boy told me. The Berlin children taught me to put principle before pleasure—to stand by what is important to you.

The children I spoke to the first time did not beg for chocolate, although they had not had any for years. They were so grateful for flour they would not ask for more. Their pride and dignity moved me, and I gave the thirty children all I had: two sticks of gum. That was just the beginning. All in all, my buddies and I ended up dropping over twenty tons of candy and gum during the next fourteen months!

Those two sticks of gum changed my life forever. I received many honors and gifts on behalf of the pilots who volunteered for the candy drops. However, all the gifts and other worldly things that resulted did not bring near the happiness and fulfillment that I received from serving others—even serving the former enemy, the Germans, who had become friends.

I had so much fun on my first drop of chocolate to the Berlin children. When I flew over the airport I could see the children down below. I wiggled my wings and the little group went crazy. I can still see their arms in the air, waving at me. I was able to give them a little candy and a little hope, but they were able to fill me up with so much more.

Thank you to all those children, and to you who are about to read their story.

Gail S. Halvorsen
The Chocolate Pilot

A Douglas C-54 Skymaster flies over Berlin to land at Tempelhof Central Airport.

1

Bread from the Heavens

Nine-year-old Peter Zimmerman searched the sky for airplanes. It was 1948, and Peter stood in his uncle's yard in West Berlin, Germany. There had been a time, three or four years earlier, when the droning of American and British bombers would have sent Peter running for cover. But World War II was over, and things had changed. Now the aircraft didn't frighten him. In fact, he longed to see a particular American plane—one that would fly over and wiggle its wings.

In the same city seven-year-old Mercedes Simon was amazed that her wartime enemies—the Americans and the British—were now her friends. She peered out the window of her apartment, watching US

As World War II ended in 1945, the Soviet army left Berlin in ruins. Here Russian soldiers walk amid the wreckage of buildings damaged or completely demolished by bombs and artillery shells.

Air Force planes swoop by to land at nearby Tempelhof Central Airport. The pounding of their mighty engines filled the air day and night. Like Peter, Mercedes was watching for a special plane—one she hoped would fly closer, rocking its wings back and forth.

West Berliners were excited to see the steady stream of great silver birds crowding their sky. Instead of bombers come to destroy, these aircraft were cargo planes that had come to save West Berliners from starvation. Each plane was filled with flour, potatoes, milk, meat, or medicine—even coal to heat homes and generate electricity for the city. Of course, there were hundreds of American and British military aviators flying into the city, but Peter and Mercedes were waiting for just one pilot. And they weren't the only ones. Every youngster in the city had an eye on the sky, waiting to spot Lt. Gail Halvorsen's plane.

But why was this pilot, along with the others, flying food into West Berlin? And why was it coming in on airplanes at all? It would have been much more efficient to transport the food with trucks and railway cars.

German civilians unload a sack of coal from a cargo plane. As the winter of 1948–49 approached, the precious fuel became as important as food.

The Reichstag (left), the traditional seat of German government, is visible across this open area used by West Berliners to plant gardens. Though gardens helped provide some fresh produce, they could supply only a fraction of the food needed for the blockaded city dwellers to survive.

The answers lie in what happened to Berlin when World War II ended in 1945. The Allied powers—Great Britain, the United States, France, and the Soviet Union (Russia)—defeated Germany and then divided it into four occupation zones. The Soviets took the northeastern part of the country, which included Berlin, the capital city. Although Britain, the United States, and France (the Western Allies) each occupied a zone, they still wanted a presence in Berlin—even though it was located 110 miles (177 kilometers) inside the Soviet-controlled zone. Therefore, the Allied powers agreed to divide up the city: the eastern part of Berlin would go to the Soviets, and the western part would be split into three sectors, one each for the Western Allies.

After World War II, the Allied powers divided Germany into four zones. They also split up Germany's capital city, Berlin. West Berlin went to France, Britain, and the United States, while East Berlin went to Russia. But Berlin lay deep in the Russian zone. When the Russians cut off land and water travel to the city, air transportation became the only way for the Western Allies to reach West Berlin.

An American cargo plane flies over Berlin as it ferries supplies into the beleaguered city. The Berlin train station, its roof blown away by bombs, can be seen to the left.

The Soviet Union had been on Germany's side earlier in the war. When Germany unexpectedly turned against Russia, the Soviets switched their allegiance and joined Britain, the United States, and France. But Russia's Communist government was a dictatorship, and it did not trust democracies. When the war ended, the Soviets distanced themselves from the democratic governments of their former allies. Soon Russia's leaders made it clear that they wanted Britain, the United States, and France out of Berlin. When they didn't leave, the Soviets cried foul by claiming that the Western Allies were forcing their democratic, capitalistic ideals on everyone in Germany.

Finally the Russians decided to drive the Westerners out by blockading Berlin—not allowing trains, cars, trucks, or river barges to reach the city. By cutting off land and water travel across the Soviet zone, the Russians intended to stop all food shipments to West Berlin. Surely after a few miserable weeks, West Berliners—who were already suffering in their war-ravaged city—would beg the Western Allies to leave so they could be fed by the Soviets. The Russians were certain Britain, the United States, and France would have no other choice but to go. As it turned out, there was another choice.

Although the treaty dividing Berlin did not guarantee travel over land and water, it did allow for several air corridors into Berlin. With this avenue of travel still open, the Western Allies decided to fly food and fuel into West Berlin in a concerted effort called the Berlin Airlift. The task was daunting. To feed over two million people seemed difficult if not impossible—certainly the Soviets thought so.

The British Royal Air Force (RAF) launched its airlift of supplies on June 26, 1948, calling it "Operation Plainfare." The RAF flew its cargo planes into Gatow Airfield in the British sector. Besides regular aircraft, it also used flying boats named Sunderlands, which had marine fuselages resistant to their corrosive payloads of salt. They landed on lakes along the River Havel in West Berlin.

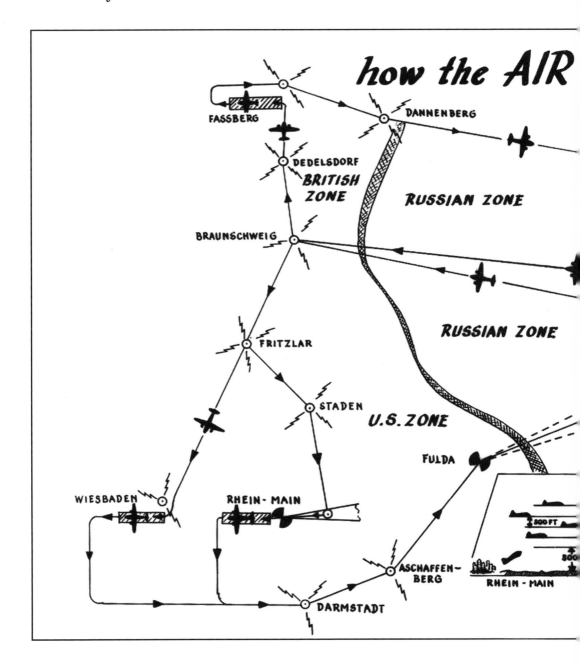

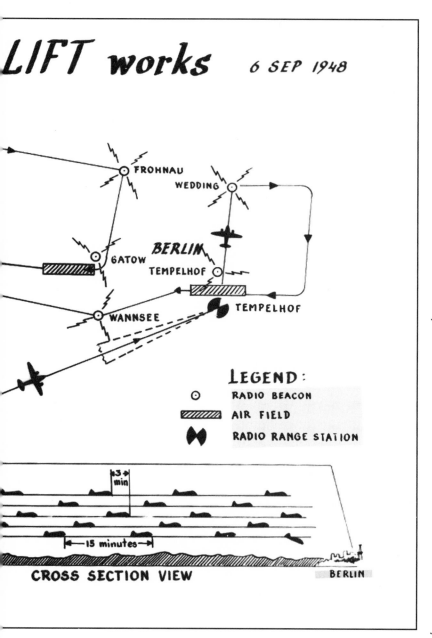

LIFT works 6 SEP 1948

FROHNAU
WEDDING
BERLIN
GATOW
TEMPELHOF
TEMPELHOF
WANNSEE

LEGEND:
⊙ RADIO BEACON
▨ AIR FIELD
▶◀ RADIO RANGE STATION

3 min
15 minutes
CROSS SECTION VIEW
BERLIN

This diagram from 1948 shows the air routes pilots used to fly into West Berlin during the Airlift. As indicated by the "cross section view," there were five different flight altitudes, which helped keep the aircraft from interfering with one another. Later, when improved navigational equipment became available, this was reduced to two flight altitudes.

Shown here in June of 1944, Lt. Gail S. Halvorsen had just graduated from flight school and received his "wings." He flew cargo planes in South America before being transferred to Rhein–Main Air Force Base in West Germany in 1948.

The Operation Vittles statistics board at Rhein-Main kept track of the tonnage airlifted by the Americans.

The US Air Force (USAF) began its airlift on the same day as the British and dubbed it "Operation Vittles," after the vittles, or food, it was flying into West Berlin. Douglas C-47 Skytrain and C-54 Skymaster aircraft flew into airfields in the French, British, and American sectors of West Berlin: Tegel, Gatow, and especially Tempelhof Central Airport. The cargo planes dropped out of the sky to land every few minutes, twenty-four hours a day. US pilots made as many flights as possible before fatigue required new flight crews to take over. One of these pilots was Gail Halvorsen, a young lieutenant who had just arrived in Germany.

In July 1948 Lt. Halvorsen arranged for a jeep tour of war-torn Berlin, during which he snapped this photograph of the Reichstag. But before he left Tempelhof to see the city, he had a fateful encounter with a group of German children—a brief visit that would change his life forever.

2

"Vhat Is Viggle?"

*L*t. Halvorsen wanted to see more of Berlin than Tempelhof's airfield, such as the bunker where Adolf Hitler had spent his last days. But the USAF cargo planes were allowed so little time on the ground that a sightseeing trip was impossible. The only option was to skip some sleep and hitch a ride on another C-54 when he was off duty. One warm day in July, Halvorsen decided to do just that. He arranged for a jeep and a driver to meet him at Tempelhof and take him into the bombed-out city.

Before the jeep arrived Lt. Halvorsen walked to the spot where the planes approached for their landings. He wanted to aim his 8 mm

A C-54 comes in over apartment buildings to land at Tempelhof. The runway was covered with temporary pierced-steel planking (visible in foreground) that made for a noisy, bone-jarring landing. The planking was later replaced with pavement.

movie camera at the war-battered apartment buildings that rose up at the end of the runway. The C-54s skimmed across the rooftops, their four propellers slicing the air as they plunged downward for a bone-jarring landing on the runway of pierced-steel planking. It was a sight worth catching on film.

As Lt. Halvorsen neared the wire fence at the end of the landing strip, he noticed a ragtag group of about thirty German children, between the ages of eight and fourteen, gathered on the other side. By the time he had filmed the first plane roaring over the chimneys, "half of the kids were right up against the fence across from me," Halvorsen remembers.

He turned, smiling at the children. "Guten Tag. Wie geht's?" ("Hello. How are you?"), he greeted them, using most of the German he knew. The youngsters not already standing at the fence rushed forward to peer through the wire, and the young pilot was inundated by a torrent of greetings in both English and German. Two or three kids emerged from the smiling, giggling group and in broken English began to ask questions for the rest.

"How many sacks of flour are on each aircraft?" one of them inquired. Lt. Halvorsen stepped closer to the fence and told them that a C-54 could carry two hundred sacks weighing a total of twenty thousand pounds (nine thousand kilograms). But as the kids peppered him with questions, the lieutenant began to understand that these young West Berliners cared about more than food.

A typical group of German kids peer through a wire fence at the end of the runway at Tempelhof.

German civilians unload sacks of flour. Each sack weighs 100 pounds (about 45 kilograms).

"We have aunts, uncles, and cousins who live in East Berlin," said one of the boys, "and they tell us how things are going for them." As the Soviets tightened their control on East Germany, they confiscated property, suppressed free speech, canceled the free elections proposed by the Western Allies, and denied a host of other civil liberties. They even went so far as to force thousands of skilled German workers to relocate to the Soviet Union.

A girl with "wistful blue eyes," wearing trousers "that looked like they belonged to an older brother," also spoke up. "Almost every one of us here experienced the final battle for Berlin," Halvorsen remembers her saying. "After your bombers had killed some of our parents, brothers, and sisters, we thought nothing could be worse. But that was before the final battle. . . . [Then] we saw firsthand the Communist system [of the Soviets]."

Here is yet another scene showing the destruction of Berlin by the Russian Army.

Lt. Halvorsen visits with German children standing behind a fence at the end of the Tempelhof runway.

Lt. Halvorsen knew these children were lucky to be alive. Frequent American bombing raids and then the final assault by Soviet troops had taken a devastating toll of lives. He knew that during the last years of the war, these same kids had scratched for what little food was available. So he was surprised to hear them say that they could get by with very little for quite a long time, as long as they could trust the Western Allies to stick by West Berlin. Though they worried about going hungry, the children seemed to agree that they were just as concerned about losing their newfound freedoms. "These young kids [gave] me the most meaningful lesson in freedom I ever had," Halvorsen recalls.

The lieutenant's eyes panned the thirty hungry faces, and his heart skipped a beat. These were the children he was here to save—children who'd grown up knowing little else but war. "I've got to go, kids," he said reluctantly. He knew the jeep was waiting to take him through the rubble-strewn streets of Berlin for more photos.

Fifty yards away from the fence, Lt. Halvorsen stopped. He couldn't get those youngsters out of his head. He knew because of the war they hadn't tasted candy in years. In other parts of the war-torn world, kids begged American servicemen for sweets, yet not one of these kids had asked him for something. He reached into his pocket and felt two sticks of Doublemint chewing gum. Turning back to the fence, he broke the sticks in half, wondering if it was a mistake to give the four puny pieces to thirty sugar-starved boys and girls.

Expecting the children to squabble over the gum, the lieutenant watched what happened in amazement: there was no fighting. The lucky four who had plucked the half sticks from his fingers kept the gum, but they ripped the wrappers into strips, passing them around so everyone could breathe in the sweet, minty smell. "In all my experience, including Christmases past," he recalls, "I had never witnessed such an expression of surprise, joy, and sheer pleasure."

Just then another C-54 roared overhead and landed, tires screeching on the runway. "The plane gave me a sudden flash of inspiration," Halvorsen remembers. "Why not drop some gum, even chocolate, to these kids out of our airplane the next daylight trip to Berlin?" Of course, the lieutenant knew he might never get permission from his commanding officer for such a stunt, but why not do it anyway? Just once. Surprising himself, Halvorsen hurried back to the fence and announced his plan to the eager children. He told them that if they would agree to share equally, he'd drop candy and chewing gum for everyone from his plane the next day.

There was excited whispering. Then after some prodding from the others, the blue-eyed girl asked how they would know which aircraft he'd be flying. That was a problem, of course. There were so many planes coming and going.

"When I get overhead, I'll wiggle the wings," said Lt. Halvorsen. It was the way he'd greeted his parents when flying a small plane over their Utah farm.

The girl wrinkled her nose in confusion. "Vhat is viggle?" she asked in her accented English.

Lt. Halvorsen held out his arms and rocked them back and forth, making the children laugh. Now that they understood the signal, some suggested he leave right away and get ready for the candy drop.

Lt. Halvorsen with the Reichstag in the background. He had just met the children at the fence and was on his sightseeing trip into war-ravaged Berlin.

West Berliners watch the skies, hoping the plane overhead will make a candy drop.

After his jeep tour of Berlin, Lt. Halvorsen hitched a ride back home to Rhein-Main Air Force Base in West Germany on an empty cargo plane. Because his next flight to Tempelhof was at 2:00 AM, he tried to get some rest. However, thoughts of candy kept him awake. American airmen received weekly ration cards to buy a few sweets, and his allotment wasn't enough for thirty kids. He needed to talk his crew into donating their rations as well. But candy was like currency in war-ravaged Germany, so they might not be willing to part with it. An airman could hire a German woman to do his weekly wash for a couple of Hershey bars. If he saved up his candy ration, he could even pick up a camera on the black market. And that was in West Germany—in Berlin, a chocolate bar had ten times the value.

Nevertheless, when Lt. Halvorsen announced his plan, his crew quickly agreed to donate their candy, even though they might be making trouble for themselves by not asking permission. But how should they go about dropping the sweets? One package, though not large, dropped at 115 miles (185 kilometers) per hour would be a dangerous missile. Halvorsen decided on three smaller packages suspended on parachutes made from handkerchiefs.

Later the next day, as the lieutenant came in for a noon landing at Tempelhof, he spotted his thirty kids waiting, necks craned to the sky. He wiggled the wings of his Douglas C-54, and they went wild, waving and cheering and running in circles.

Candy parachutes scatter from a C-54. Though Halvorsen initially jettisoned only three candy-laden handkerchiefs, later drops released hundreds or even thousands of parachutes at a time.

"Now!" Lt. Halvorsen cried to Sergeant Elkins, the crew chief, who thrust the three handkerchiefs into the tube for releasing emergency flares. The little parachutes shot out of the tube "like popcorn." But had the candy drifted lazily into eager fingers or settled on roofs or even on the runway?

The answer came a few minutes later. Soon after German volunteers had emptied the Skymaster's cargo hold of its flour, Halvorsen started up the engines. The steady stream of air traffic demanded a

Lieutenant Gail Halvorsen, Technical Sergeant Herschel C. Elkins, and Captain John H. Pickering made the first candy drops to the children at the end of the runway at Tempelhof.

With cargo planes landing as frequently as every ten minutes, both loading the aircraft and unloading them had to be accomplished swiftly. This photograph shows coal-hauling C-54s being loaded at Gatow Airfield.

quick turnaround—unload and get back in the air. As their plane rumbled down the taxi strip, the crew spotted three white handkerchiefs fluttering through the wire fence.

"The little parachutes were being waved . . . at every crew as each aircraft taxied by," Halvorsen recalls. "Behind the three with the parachutes were the rest of the cheering section with both arms waving above their heads and every jaw working on a prize."

Lt. Halvorsen holds an armload of silk parachutes given to him by a supply officer.

3

Operation Little Vittles

During the next two weeks Lt. Halvorsen and his crew made two more drops to the kids, who waited patiently until they spotted the plane with the wiggling wings. The group at the end of the runway swelled in size each time. Then the mail began to pour into Tempelhof Central Airport: letters addressed to Onkel Wackelflügel (Uncle Wiggly Wings) or Der Schokoladen-flieger (The Chocolate Pilot). All the publicity made the crew nervous. "Holy cow!" Lt. Halvorsen exclaimed when he first laid eyes on the stacks of envelopes waiting for him at Tempelhof. Now he was certain trouble was knocking at the door. The sheer volume of mail was enough to tip off his superior officers about the candy drops. So Halvorsen and the rest of the crew decided that the next load of six parachutes would be their last—but it was already too late.

The day after what they thought was their last candy drop, the commanding officer summoned Halvorsen to his office at Rhein-Main Air Force Base. "What in the world have you been doing?" Colonel Haun demanded. He plopped a newspaper from Frankfurt, Germany, on the desk. "You almost hit a reporter in the head with a candy bar in Berlin yesterday. He's spread the story all over Europe."

Standing before the peeved superior officer, Lt. Halvorsen thought his flying days might be over. Then Colonel Haun said, "The general called me with congratulations, and I didn't know anything about it. Why didn't you tell me?"

The reporter had nicknamed the candy drops "Operation Little Vittles" and praised the pilot's efforts. Apparently the US Air Force loved the good publicity, because Lt. Halvorsen was ordered to appear at an upcoming international press conference. The colonel was only upset that General Tunner had caught him off guard. "Keep flying," he told Halvorsen, "keep dropping, and keep me informed."

Soon after, the Air Force officially adopted the name "Operation Little Vittles" for the candy drops and provided two German secretaries to help deal with the mountain of fan mail. Other servicemen began donating their sweets rations; Halvorsen would return to his quarters to find his cot covered with candy, gum, and hankies to use

In the beginning Halvorsen's fellow airmen kept Operation Little Vittles going by contributing their candy rations and handkerchiefs.

The Berlin Airlift dominated the attention of even the very young. Here young West Berliners act out the daily events at Tempelhof. They have laid out the bricks in the configuration of the buildings at the airport.

for parachutes. When they ran out of hankies, they started using shirt-tails. Shirtsleeves were lopped off and sewed at one end to make candy bags to suspend from the parachutes.

A supply officer provided a dozen small, silk parachutes (one yard—about one meter—in diameter), which could carry a much heavier load of candy and gum. They were too nice to use only once, so they were inscribed in German with the message: "Please return this parachute to any American Military Policeman that you see so it may be used again." There was also an English message: "Please return this parachute to Tempelhof Base Operations for Operation Little Vittles."

Fabric was nearly as scarce as food, so other pilots said Halvorsen would never see the silk parachutes again—they'd be made into underwear and shirts. However, the first time they were dropped, six came back to Tempelhof the same day. Not only did children and their parents usually return the silk parachutes, but they also often enclosed with their letters the smaller parachutes they'd caught or ones they'd made themselves.

It didn't take long for the crowds of kids—and their parents—at the end of the runway at Tempelhof to grow too large and, therefore, too dangerous. Lt. Halvorsen worried the youngsters might trample

Little Vittles parachutes descend over a crowd waiting near Tempelhof.

one another—or be trampled by adults—in their "mad dash" for the candy. So he changed the parachute drops to random spots all over West Berlin, such as parks, playgrounds, cemeteries, and schoolyards. This led to letters from East Berlin children. Because the Berlin Wall, which later separated East from West, didn't yet exist, children in the Soviet sector were dashing across the boundary to snag a few parachutes themselves. They wrote to Uncle Wiggly Wings, asking to be included. After all, "you have to fly right over us before you turn to land," they said. "There are parks and schoolyards that would make good targets over here." So Halvorsen did it—at least, for two weeks.

It didn't take the Soviets long to figure out what was happening. They lodged a formal complaint with the US State Department, claiming the East Berlin candy drops were a "capitalist trick to influence the minds of young people." In order to avoid further trouble with Russia, the Air Force ordered the lieutenant to stop making drops over the Soviet sector of the city. However, one girl managed to grab thirteen parachutes before the ban went into place.

The mountains of letters arriving at Tempelhof included word from the polio hospital in West Berlin. Children suffering from the crippling disease guaranteed the Chocolate Pilot that their nurses and doctors wouldn't mind a noisy, low-level flight over the hospital. The doctors even promised to catch the parachutes and bring them inside to the kids. They said the "fun of Little Vittles was better medicine than anything they had." But Halvorsen did not attempt a candy

drop to the young polio patients because the hospital was located out-
side approved flight paths. Instead, he arranged to visit the children in
person. By that time individuals and companies from the United
States were starting to donate larger quantities of candy, and a case of
Paris-brand bubble gum had just arrived. Most German kids had
never seen bubble gum, so Lt. Halvorsen took the whole case to them,
along with lots of chocolate.

*As word of Operation Little Vittles spread, donations of candy and parachute
materials poured in from many sources, especially from back home in the
United States. This photograph shows a large box of Paris bubble gum that
Lt. Halvorsen took with him to the polio hospital in West Berlin.*

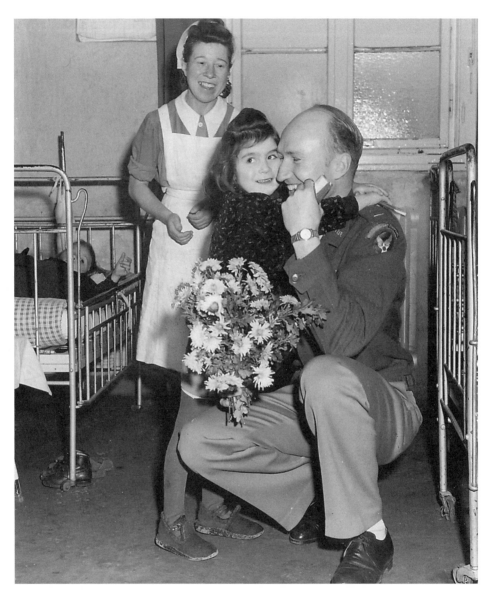

Lt. Halvorsen receives a hug and a bouquet from a young patient at the polio hospital.

James Gibson demonstrates the art of blowing bubbles for children in the hospital. Like most German kids, they had never before seen bubble gum.

The lieutenant was never much of a bubble blower, so he wondered how best to show the kids what bubble gum was all about. Then an American health officer, James Gibson, admitted that he had been something of a bubble-blowing champion in his day. He put on quite a demonstration. Learning to blow bubbles was a big hit, and the hospital halls echoed with snaps and pops for days to come. The joy that came from the bubble gum encouraged the German nurses to set aside their worries about sticky sheets and pillowcases.

*Before joining the US Army Air Corps (which later became the US Air Force),
Gail Halvorsen worked on his family's farm in Garland, Utah. Here he poses
with his dogs and his 1924 Maxwell automobile. (1939)*

— 4 —

From Little Things Come Big Things

No matter how far the Air Force took Gail Halvorsen from his boyhood home on a farm in Utah, the values he learned from his salt-of-the-earth parents never left him. One of the nuggets of wisdom he remembered hearing from his father proved out during his time in Germany: "From little things come big things."

Of his experiences with Operation Little Vittles, Halvorsen has said more than once that two sticks of gum, passed through a wire fence in Berlin, brought about something larger and more important than he could have imagined. In fact, what came out of this small act captured the interest and attention of the world, making it possible to multiply the effects of Operation Little Vittles a thousandfold.

At first contributions to the candy drops started coming in from Armed Forces personnel living in West Germany. Then supplies began arriving from England and the United States, and from as far away as Australia. Because radio stations in the United States offered to play requests if listeners sent hankies to Uncle Wiggly Wings, letters with parachutes poured into the mailroom at Rhein-Main Air Force Base where Halvorsen was stationed. (Because Lt. Halvorsen was a bachelor, some were perfumed and trimmed with lace!) *Weekly Reader*, the popular classroom newspaper, also urged students to send handkerchiefs. Many American children who sent hankies requested names and addresses for West Berlin pen pals.

Lt. Halvorsen opens mail from Little Vittles supporters. Behind him are boxes of donated Hershey bars.

An old Chicopee, Massachusetts, fire station became the Center for Operation Little Vittles in the United States. The center shipped tons of supplies donated by individuals and businesses.

In an old fire station in Chicopee, Massachusetts, a group of supporters formed the "Center for Operation Little Vittles." Local schools—twenty-two of them—and businesses banded together to gather and contribute supplies. Chaired by college student Mary Connors, the center became a massive operation. By January of 1949 it was shipping eight hundred pounds (more than three hundred kilograms) of supplies to West Germany every other day. Businesses and individuals donated eighteen tons (sixteen thousand kilograms) of candy and gum, and two thousand sheets, three thousand hankies, and eleven thousand yards of ribbon for parachutes.

In November of 1948, when newspapers reported the ban on dropping candy over East Berlin, increased support poured in from across the United States. A news article recounted some of the donations:

Latest developments in the amazing growth of . . . [Operation Little Vittles] include the following: a donation of 900 pounds of twine . . . , a gift of 1,100 yards of linen to make parachutes . . . , [and] another large gift of cloth for the same purpose. The kids will stamp the following message on each parachute: "This candy is sent to you from the school children of America." The message will be in German. (From the Springfield Massachusetts Union, *November 2, 1948.)*

About this time Lt. Halvorsen was suddenly in demand for appearances back in the United States, and General Tunner sent him to New York City for television, radio, and newspaper interviews. After

LIFE SAVERS
Corporation
Executive Offices and Main Factory
PORT CHESTER, N.Y.

October 21, 1948.

Lt. Dale Halvorsen.
Operation Little Vittles.
Westover Field, Mass.

Dear Lt. Halvorsen:

We have just received a memorandum from Mr. E.E. Anderson, one of our directors, telling us about the very unique brand of thoughtfulness that you are showering on the Berlin children. It goes without saying that generosity as free of provisos and conditions as yours deserves loud applause.

We join all others the world over who have heard of your enterprise and hope for its continuance. We are pleased to donate our share of this savory jetsam and have therefore arranged to ship you 200 boxes of Life Savers, in all, some 4,000 rolls.

In order that our share of the cargo be distributed at peak freshness, we plan to ship you 1,000 rolls of Life Savers during the next week and follow this up with successive shipment of the same quantity at your request.

Just notify us by card as often as you have cargo space and we will send our product forward within a week of your request. Again, we wish you and "Little Vittles" continued success and assure you of our continued cooperation.

Yours very truly,

LIFE SAVERS Corp.,

John G. Burnett

JBurnett;f   Advertising Department.

Candy companies got into the act. Here is a letter from Life Savers, offering to send 200 boxes of their product, adding up to more than 4,000 rolls.

the interviews John Swersey from the American Confectioners Association, an organization of candy companies, invited the lieutenant to lunch. The farm boy had never been at a table set with four forks at each plate, so he was a little overwhelmed. Then, in the midst of this extravagant meal, Mr. Swersey looked up and asked, "How much of this stuff can you use?" He went on to say that the members of his organization were excited about Operation Little Vittles and wanted to do more to help. Lt. Halvorsen was so surprised that afterward he couldn't recall the amount of candy he'd requested, but in little more than a month, 6,500 pounds (2,900 kilograms) of sweets arrived in Germany—enough to fill two railroad boxcars.

Halvorsen and his accomplices had too much to drop by parachute, so they arranged to have the candy and gum transported by plane to West Berlin. There it was locked up in a jail cell and guarded, as it was worth a small fortune on the black market. The candy sat in the cell for two or three weeks until Christmas. On the afternoon of Christmas Eve, the German Youth Association and the US military threw several big parties for the kids of West Berlin and gave the candy away.

Lt. Halvorsen wasn't able to attend the celebrations. Instead, he was in the air, flying loads of potatoes, eggs, and flour into West Berlin. As he circled above the blockaded city, the lieutenant smiled as he imagined throngs of kids munching on candy by the handful.

Newspapers across the United States continued to run stories about Operation Little Vittles, and with every news article, more

The German Youth Association, shown here in a publicity photograph, helped distribute thousands of pounds of candy flown into West Berlin for Christmas parties in 1948.

A German family shares the "sky-food" dropped by an Operation Little Vittles crew.

Two representatives from the Non-commissioned Officers' Wives Club meet with Halvorsen at the Rhein-Main Community Center to help organize the increasing number of candy drops.

letters and contributions rolled in. Despite the mass candy giveaways at the Christmas parties, there was still enough for every pilot willing to drop parachutes. In fact, so many were involved that Operation Little Vittles needed organizational help in order to keep the candy moving. The Officers' Wives Club and the Non-commissioned Officers' Wives Club at Rhein-Main Air Force Base pitched in to do the job. They displayed a large map of Berlin in the Operations Office, along with boxes of candy-laden parachutes. Numbers on the boxes corresponded with coordinates on the map, helping to guarantee that the city would be evenly covered.

Many children sent drawings that depicted the candy drops.

5

"Dear Onkl of the Heaven"

By October of 1948 Peter Zimmerman must have decided he'd never score a candy parachute unless he took matters into his own hands. So he sent a letter—in English—to the man he hoped would soon be his Chocolate Uncle. He also tucked a map and a crude homemade parachute into the envelope. "As you see," he wrote, "after take off fly along the big canal to the second highway bridge, turn right one block. I live in the bombed-out house on the corner. I'll be in the backyard every day at 2 PM. Drop the chocolate there."

Lt. Halvorsen followed the map, spotted kids waiting below, and released the parachutes. A week later another letter from a frustrated

Peter arrived: "Didn't get any gum or candy, a bigger kid beat me to it," he complained. Of course, it was nearly impossible for Uncle Wiggly Wings to drop a parachute directly into Peter's backyard. More than once, he failed to get any goodies into the boy's hands, and this was made quite clear by yet another letter. On a page with a handsomely drawn airplane dropping candy-laden parachutes, Peter wrote, "Have not received any chocolate yet!" Still, he thanked Halvorsen for his "good will" and enclosed some additional drawings as a way of showing his gratitude for the American pilot's efforts.

On the tarmac at Rhein-Main, Halvorsen demonstrates how candy-laden parachutes are dropped from a C-54.

Have not Ecaivedany chocolate yet!

Aut I aln want thank you for your good will and Han!

Here tam precsenting you a few draws in Emelzrance to

Berlin
and me!

In this letter, Peter Zimmerman complains that he has missed out on the chocolate so far. Notice that the message on the tail of the plane says, "No chocolate yet."

Peter Zimmerman usually sent artwork with his letters to Uncle Wiggly Wings.

Lt. Halvorsen's drops to Peter were never successful, so Peter's patience wore thin. In a letter without the gift of his artwork enclosed, he chided the American flyer: "You are a pilot? I gave you a map. How did you guys win the war?" He even suggested he might build a fire so the smoke would guide the plane—then Uncle Wiggly Wings could drop the candy upwind. After that letter Lt. Halvorsen decided not to risk missing his target again. He loaded a package with chocolate and gum and mailed it to Peter.

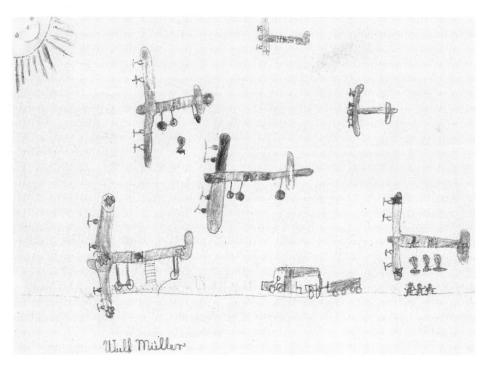

This child's drawing shows not only the candy drops, but also the delivery of food supplies.

The post office also proved to be the only way to fulfill the request in Mercedes Simon's letter. "My dear chocolate uncle," Mercedes wrote in German. "We live near the airfield at Tempelhof and our chickens think your airplanes are chicken hawks, and they become frightened when you fly over to land. They run in the shelter, and some molt and give us no more eggs." However, Mercedes knew a way to offset the tragedy of unhappy hens that wouldn't lay eggs. She concluded her letter by saying, "When you see the white chickens please drop [the chocolate] there, all will be OK." But Lt. Halvorsen was never able to find the white chickens from the air and ended up mailing the candy to Mercedes.

Like Peter Zimmerman, Peter Petri wasn't big enough to compete for the parachutes. "Dear Onkl of the Heaven," he wrote in awkward English, "I'll often standing on the park of Neukolln and waiting for something of you. But I'll never couldn't catch anything cause I am not big enough. The children of 12–14 years old, and the people pick the best stuff up. But what's to do? Can you help me?"

Of course, not all the letters were requests for special candy runs; most were letters of gratitude. Sometimes the thank-you notes included humorous stories about the perils of catching parachutes. For example, Klaus Rickowski wrote that he jumped into a duck pond to retrieve a parachute. When he climbed out he was covered with mud, algae, and duck manure. He continued on to school, arriving late and in a smelly and sodden condition. Klaus's usually strict teacher overlooked his tardiness and sent him home to change.

Mercedes Simon wrote to Lt. Halvorsen about her chickens that stopped laying eggs because of the noisy C-54s flying overhead. In this picture, taken the year before the Airlift began, Mercedes poses on the first day of school. Her shoes, purchased on the black market, are of the same style but are two different sizes.

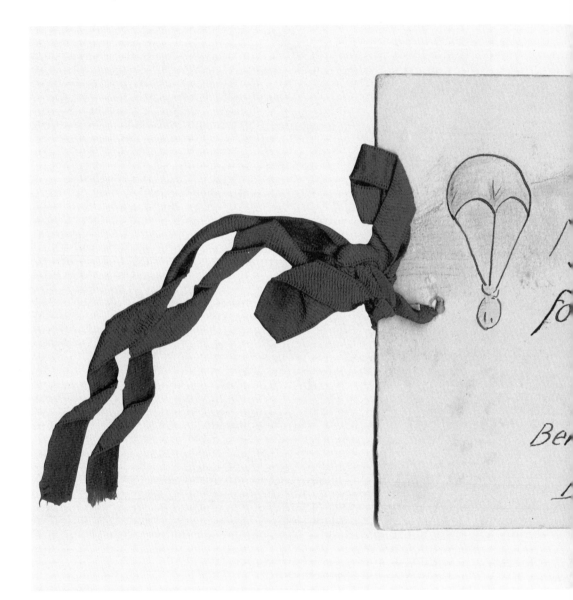

Here is an example of the many thank-yous regularly received by Gail Halvorsen from grateful children in Berlin.

best thanks

he „Sky-Food",

Rose-Mary Fricke

-Schöneberg, Gustav-Müller-Platz 1

lin, 14ᵗᵉⁿ okt. 1948.

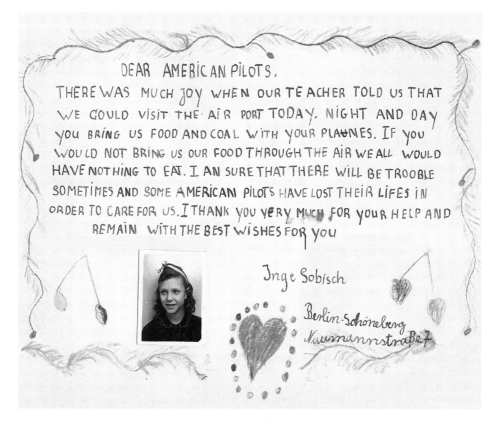

DEAR AMERICAN PILOTS,
THERE WAS MUCH JOY WHEN OUR TEACHER TOLD US THAT
WE COULD VISIT THE AIR PORT TODAY. NIGHT AND DAY
YOU BRING US FOOD AND COAL WITH YOUR PLAUNES. IF YOU
WOULD NOT BRING US OUR FOOD THROUGH THE AIR WE ALL WOULD
HAVE NOTHING TO EAT. I AN SURE THAT THERE WILL BE TROOBLE
SOMETIMES AND SOME AMERICAN PILOTS HAVE LOST THEIR LIFES IN
ORDER TO CARE FOR US. I THANK YOU VERY MUCH FOR YOUR HELP AND
REMAIN WITH THE BEST WISHES FOR YOU

Inge Sobisch

Berlin-Schöneberg
Naumannstraße 7

Often the pilots would receive letters thanking them not for the candy but for the food, fuel, and medicine that kept West Berliners alive. Here is a thoughtful letter, complete with drawings and a photograph of the sender.

Other letters were less humorous and far more poignant. A West Berlin father wrote to say he had nothing, absolutely nothing, to give his son for his birthday. He tried in vain to carve a little horse from wood, noting that his miserable failure proved that—contrary to common belief—not all Germans are great wood-carvers. Then, from his window, the father spotted a smudge of white against the gray roof. Hands trembling, he used a stick to rake in the parachute and his son's birthday gift.

Scraping up something for birthdays seemed a widespread problem. Another parent sent a letter thanking Lt. Halvorsen for providing the only present her son received when he turned sixteen. "It was the first sweets for the children in a very long time," Helga Müller wrote. "Chocolate can't be bought even with money." In fact, sweets were so precious that "if there was only one chewing gum, it would be passed from mouth to mouth," Inge Tscherner recalled years later in a letter to Halvorsen. "Everyone was allowed to chew 10 times."

Adults and children alike addressed Lt. Halvorsen with a variety of affectionate names in their letters: "Dear Angel from the Sky," "Dear Chocolate Uncle," "Dear Uncle from Heaven," "Dear Aviator of Chocolate," "Dear Mr. Candy Bomber," "Dear Flying Chocolate-Officer," "Dear Bonbon Pilot," and, of course, "Dear Uncle Wiggly Wings." Some letters began simply with "Dear Lt. Halvorsen." One such note arrived from Gertraud and Brigitte Schuffelhauer. "We live in Charlottenburg," they wrote, "and cannot to Tempelhof come. My sister and I like so much chocolate to eat, but our mother can us not buy and our father is dead. Please perhaps one time something for us to bring?"

By December not only Lt. Halvorsen but also every Berlin Airlift pilot was a hero to the kids of West Berlin. It was commonplace to

On October 15, 1948, Elly Muss wrote a pleading letter to the "Schokoladen Flieger" (Chocolate Pilot). "For days and days, four small brothers <u>without a father</u> have run to the airport in vain to get their hardworking mother a piece of chocolate," Elly wrote. "Is there another way to fulfill this request for five hungry souls?" She included this photo and provided her return address. The air-base secretaries who helped handle Operation Little Vittles mail saw to it that the request was "fulfilled."

see children crossing the ramp at Tempelhof or one of the other airfields to greet their benefactors. Followed by a parent, the youngsters would shyly approach the pilots and present them with armloads of fresh flowers that had somehow surfaced in the bombed-out city even in the dead of winter. Halvorsen recalls watching two little girls,

Lt. Halvorsen received a letter from Trugard Brunger asking for his help. "Our little children . . . only get poor . . . milk powder, which they cannot drink but only eat on their bread. . . . Is it possible to bring us better powdered milk during the Blockade?" Eventually, shipments of fresh milk came in on the cargo planes. Perhaps other than the chocolate and gum, it was the cargo most appreciated by the children of West Berlin.

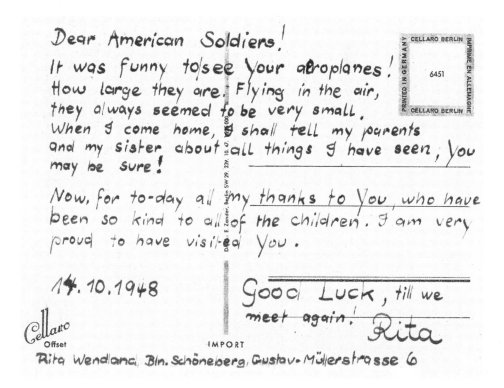

Dear American Soldiers!
It was funny to/see your aeroplanes!
How large they are. Flying in the air,
they always seemed to be very small.
When I come home, I shall tell my parents
and my sister about all things I have seen, you
may be sure!

Now, for to-day all my thanks to you, who have
been so kind to all of the children. I am very
proud to have visited you.

14.10.1948

Good Luck, till we
meet again! Rita

Rita Wendland, Bln. Schöneberg, Gustav-Müllerstrasse 6

Children in West Berlin sometimes visited the airfields to see the cargo planes and meet the airmen. Afterward, they often wrote thank-you notes.

bundled in their winter coats and trailed by their grandmother, hurrying across the wind-blown airfield. Smiling, they curtsied to the surprised American flyers, handed them a colorful reminder of summer's glory, and then skipped happily away.

Of all the Airlift pilots Halvorsen was arguably the most popular. All the press coverage had made him something of a celebrity. He received his fair share of thank-you bouquets—and other gifts as well.

Children greet Lt. Halvorsen at Tempelhof.

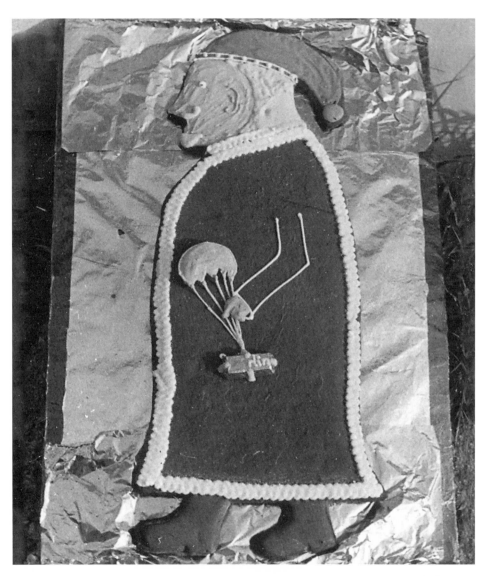

Irene Oppermann and her mother baked Lt. Halvorsen a gingerbread Saint Nicholas and delivered it to him at Tempelhof. Note that St. Nick is holding a parachute from which is suspended a candy bar.

For instance, Manfred and Klaus Meisner scrounged broken pieces of marble from the destroyed Reichstag (Germany's parliament building), shaping and polishing them into a fine set of bookends for Lt. Halvorsen. Then before Christmas Irene Oppermann and her mother baked him a gingerbread Saint Nicholas carrying a candy-laden parachute.

The most touching gift came from a little girl who handed him her most cherished possession—a brown Berlin teddy bear with fur worn thin. It had been her comfort in the dark cellar during the American and British bombing raids. "Take good care of him for me," she said, eyes welling with tears. Although the American pilot tried to return her prized, fuzzy friend, the girl would have none of it.

These outpourings of gratitude had their roots in something deeper than chocolate, as expressed by one of the children years later. He remembered walking to school one day when he was ten. Through the clouds and drizzle he could hear but not see the planes landing at Tempelhof. "Suddenly, out of the mist came a parachute with a fresh Hershey chocolate bar from America," he recalled. "It took me a week to eat that candy bar. I hid it day and night. The chocolate was wonderful, but it wasn't the chocolate that was most important. What it meant was that someone in America cared. That parachute was something more important than candy. It represented hope. Hope that someday we would be free. Without hope the soul dies."

After Lt. Halvorsen left Germany, the work of Operation Little Vittles
was continued by Capt. Eugene Williams, who produced this flyer in 1949.
Williams is pictured on the upper left and Halvorsen on the lower left.

6

Ties That Are Never Broken

As 1948 drew to a close, the US Air Force informed Lt. Halvorsen that his rotation time had come. His new assignment was to fly the larger C-74 cargo planes out of Brookley Air Force Base in Mobile, Alabama. While he prepared to leave, some must have wondered what would happen to Operation Little Vittles without Uncle Wiggly Wings.

As he flew out of Rhein-Main in January of 1949, heading home to the United States, Halvorsen wasn't a bit worried about the candy drops. He had left them in good hands. For the first month Captain Larry Caskey would head the operations. Then Captain Eugene T.

"Willy" Williams, an ardent supporter of Operation Little Vittles, would take charge.

As it turned out, not only did Willy continue the work, but he and the other pilots also increased the payload as more planes took to the air. For example, on Easter Sunday in 1949, a plane landed almost every sixty seconds, setting a one-day record of 1,398 flights that transported 12,940 tons (11,740,000 kilograms) of food and supplies. With the rise in the number of flights and a growing number of Little Vittles volunteers, Willy ended up dropping more candy by the time the Berlin Airlift ended than Uncle Wiggly Wings and Captain Caskey combined.

In May 1949 the Soviets finally acknowledged that the Airlift was unstoppable and lifted the blockade on Berlin. Although transports by train, truck, and barge were now allowed, the Airlift continued until September 30. The Western Allies weren't certain the Russians would stick to their agreement, so they continued airlifting supplies into the city until enough food and fuel were stockpiled—just in case the Soviets changed their minds.

During the sixteen months of the Berlin Airlift, seventy USAF and Royal Air Force personnel lost their lives in plane crashes and other accidents, especially during the brutal winter weather. Many civilians died aiding the Airlift, as well, but at least the sacrifices had been meaningful. As the titan effort ended, the staggering payload totals were a measure of the millions of lives saved. Pilots and their crews

Capt. Williams, the new chief of Operation Little Vittles, drops a large container of candy parachutes over West Berlin.

The Berlin Airlift was not without its casualties, as shown in this photograph of a crash. Winter weather was especially treacherous for the pilots.

made 277,569 flights into West Berlin to deliver food, coal, and liquid fuel totaling 2,325,510 tons (2,109,670,000 kilograms). Not included in those numbers were the tons of candy and gum delivered by Uncle Wiggly Wings and Operation Little Vittles.

As Gail Halvorsen left Germany behind and moved ahead with his life, one thing didn't change: he stayed in the US Air Force and made it his lifetime career. But even as the years passed and he moved up the ranks to Colonel, Halvorsen's connections with the children of West Berlin were never really severed.

US airmen and German civilians celebrate the end of the Berlin Airlift on September 30, 1949.

For example, Mae and Ernie Jantzen contacted Colonel Halvorsen while he was assigned to the Pentagon in Washington, DC, and asked if they might have the privilege of taking him and his wife to dinner. During the evening out, the Jantzens revealed that they had responded to a radio station's offer to play requested tunes for those who would send parachutes to Operation Little Vittles. "We sent you three

Lt. Halvorsen proposes to his future wife, Alta Jolley. The engagement ring is in the payload of the Little Vittles parachute in his hands. (February 1949)

Lt. Halvorsen, accompanied by his wife, accepts the 1948 Cheney Award "in recognition of . . . self-sacrifice in the humanitarian interest." Secretary of the Air Force Stewart Symington stands to Halvorsen's left. General Hoyt Vandenberg is on Mrs. Halvorsen's right. (May 1949)

with our names and addresses on them," they said. "In a couple of weeks we received replies from two of the kids who caught them." Mae and Ernie, who could not have children of their own, informally adopted the two children, sending a total of seventy-seven care packages over the following years. They even provided the wedding dress for the little girl when she grew up and was married—and later formula for her baby. "These kids blessed our lives," said Mae. "They were an answer to a prayer, and all for such a little thing as three handkerchiefs!"

In July of 1969 the Pentagon telephoned Halvorsen, who was then a commander at Vandenberg Air Force Base in California. The voice on the other end of the telephone said, "Those kids who caught your parachutes in 1948 and 1949 have gone to the Air Force Colonel commanding Tempelhof . . . and told him their kids want to see what it is like to catch those parachutes."

Tempelhof was still operating as an American air base, and once a year the Air Force opened it to Berliners, who came to see the cargo planes and remember how their city was saved (plus eat American hamburgers and ice cream). "Now they want you to come and drop goodies to their kids during the celebration," the caller said. "Will you do it?"

Colonel Halvorsen was on his way in no time. He sent ahead a list of names from the letters German children had written him, and Air Force personnel found many of them. Halvorsen and the "children"—now adults, of course—had a grand lunch together, swapping stories and laughing over the letters and pictures he'd received from them. He was thrilled to join the flight line again and soar over Berlin, dropping candy parachutes to a new generation. "The kids ran just as fast as ever," he recalls.

Colonel Halvorsen dumps candy parachutes from a C–47 Skytrain over Berlin in 1969, during a twenty-year commemoration celebration of the Airlift.

Halvorsen surrounded by the children of the children who caught his parachutes in 1948. (July 1969)

Even with the reenactment of his candy drops still fresh in his mind, Gail Halvorsen couldn't have expected what happened next. A few months later, just before Christmas, another call came from Washington, DC. The Air Force had a new assignment for him— Commander at Tempelhof in Berlin.

Gail Halvorsen's return to Berlin in 1970 opened wide the door to reconnecting with the children from 1948. Again he represented all his Air Force buddies who had been part of Operation Little Vittles. "Almost everyone who caught a parachute wanted us to come to dinner," he remembers. It was during this tour of duty that he learned for the first time that some children of Russian military personnel in East Berlin had also nabbed a few parachutes.

Sitting at his desk at Tempelhof, Colonel Halvorsen recalls Operations Vittles and Little Vittles.

Of course, it was impossible to accept all the dinner invitations, but the genuine nature of one insistent invitation finally caught the colonel's attention. He and his family canceled an official engagement and made their way to an old apartment building on Hähnelstrasse, not far from Tempelhof. A young couple and their two sons welcomed them at the door. Ushering them inside, the boys' mother retrieved an old envelope and handed it to Halvorsen. "Read this," she said, her voice trembling.

As he unfolded the page, he recognized his own signature. The letter was dated November 4, 1948, and the words, typewritten in German by a secretary, read:

> *My dear Mercedes,*
>
> *Thank you for your little letter. I don't fly over your house every day but surely quite often.*
>
> *I didn't know that in Hähnelstrasse there lived such a nice little girl. If I could fly a few rounds over [your neighborhood], I surely would find the garden with the white chickens, but there is not enough time for this.*
>
> *I hope I can give you a little joy with what accompanies this letter.*
>
> *Affectionate greetings,*
> *Your Chocolate Uncle*
> *Gail Halvorsen*

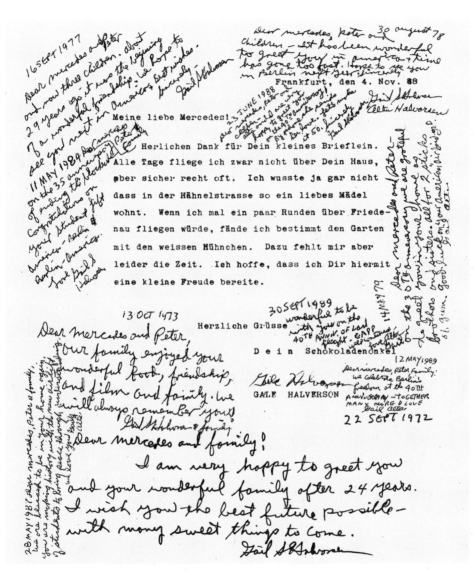

Here is the letter Lt. Halvorsen wrote to Mercedes Simon in 1948. After finally meeting Mercedes in 1972, Halvorsen began adding a note to the letter with each subsequent visit.

Colonel Halvorsen stands next to a C-54 with Mercedes Simon Wild, her husband, Peter, and their two sons.

"I carefully rationed the candy and gum and ate it little by little," explained Mercedes, "but I will keep the letter forever." Then stepping to the same window she had peered through as a little girl, she pointed out the small backyard that had once held her elusive white chickens.

Although many years have passed since the Berlin Airlift—and even since Uncle Wiggly Wings finally met the little girl with the frightened chickens—the memory of candy parachutes hasn't faded from German memory. As the days of the 2002 Winter Olympic Games approached, the telephone rang at eighty-year-old Gail Halvorsen's home in Spanish Fork, Utah. "We would like you to lead the German Olympic Team into Eccles Stadium for the opening and closing ceremonies," said the caller. "Will you do it?" Stunned, Halvorsen accepted the once-in-a-lifetime opportunity.

On a frigid February evening, retired Colonel Gail S. Halvorsen marched into Salt Lake City's Olympic Stadium, leading Germany's athletes. He wondered if some of those following him might be grandchildren, or even great-grandchildren, of the youngsters he had helped to feed in 1948 and 1949. "The image of that destroyed city under my C-54 wings came back to me in a flood of . . . memories," he recalls. "My feelings . . . [were] beyond my ability to express." The children of war-torn Berlin hadn't forgotten the young pilot and his friends who'd once given them hope in the guise of a chocolate bar.

A new generation of children, the kids of the kids from 1948–49, scrambles after candy parachutes dropped by Halvorsen to commemorate the twentieth anniversary of the Berlin Airlift. (July 1969)

Lt. Gail Halvorsen stands next to the landing gear of a Douglas C-54 Skymaster on the tarmac at Rhein-Main. He is holding one of the first three parachutes to be dropped to the children of West Berlin. (July 1948)

Biographical Note

*G*ail Halvorsen's fame as the originator of Operation Little Vittles has followed him throughout his life. Now in his eighties Halvorsen continues to receive accolades for his candy bombing during the Berlin Airlift.

Halvorsen has also participated in candy drops at schools and in other humanitarian airlift efforts around the world. These activities began the moment Halvorsen returned to the United States in 1949. His hometown, Garland, Utah, threw a two-day celebration to welcome him back, and the festivities included a candy drop from a C-47 flying over Main Street. "The only casualty was a little girl . . .

Home on leave, Lt. Halvorsen flies over Garland, Utah, dropping candy parachutes to a crowd on Main Street. (February 26, 1949)

[whose] lollipop came loose and gave her a scratch on the head," Halvorsen remembers.

Since his days as Base Commander at Tempelhof, he has returned to Germany for many Airlift-related events. In 1985 he was there when the grade school at Rhein-Main Air Force Base was christened with a new name: Gail S. Halvorsen Elementary School. Then

Halvorsen was back in Berlin on September 30, 1989, for the fortieth anniversary of the Airlift's final day. Two of his sons joined him in a large C-130 cargo plane as he dropped candy parachutes over the city. Among the children who chased after the treats were four of Mercedes Simon Wild's children, three of Gail Halvorsen's children, and seven of his grandchildren.

Halvorsen's first opportunity for another humanitarian airlift experience came in 1994. The Air Force allowed him to participate in

Gail Halvorsen prepares to drop a candy parachute from a US Army helicopter as part of the fortieth-anniversary celebration of the Berlin Airlift. (September 1989)

Operation Provide Promise, a three-and-a-half-year relief mission to refugees in Bosnia and Herzegovina. Serbia (one of the former Yugoslavian republics) had ignited age-old ethnic hostilities that erupted into civil war in this region of Eastern Europe. Nearly two million homeless refugees from Bosnia-Herzegovina and Croatia (also former Yugoslavian republics) had to flee the war-torn area.

A spry seventy-three-year-old Halvorsen joined the crew of a C-130 flying from Germany to Bosnia. Unlike in the Berlin Airlift, this plane didn't land to unload. Instead, it parachuted several giant pallets, each holding 3,500 pounds (1,600 kilograms) of supplies. A cardboard box filled with candy parachutes was fastened to the last pallet, and they scattered as it dropped away from the plane.

Since the Bosnia drop Gail Halvorsen has continued to be involved in a variety of events related to the Berlin Airlift. In 1995 NASA took a candy parachute from 1948 on the Space Shuttle. When the Shuttle docked with the Russian space station, *Mir*, an astronaut snapped a photograph of a Russian cosmonaut and an American astronaut holding the parachute between them.

In 1994 the Berlin Airlift Historical Foundation completed restoration of a C-54 and dubbed it the *Spirit of Freedom*. The plane became a flying museum of the Berlin Airlift, which Halvorsen has flown to many locations for display. In 1998 he joined the crew to pilot the *Spirit of Freedom* to Berlin for the fiftieth anniversary of the beginning of the Airlift.

Timothy Chopp, founder of the Berlin Airlift Historical Foundation, and Gail Halvorsen serve as pilot and copilot of the Spirit of Freedom. *(1998)*

On the way over, the plane stopped at Westover Air Force Base near Chicopee, Massachusetts, where it was met with band music and by a crowd of eight hundred school kids. Also in the gathering were a few people who had packed candy and tied up parachutes at the Center for Operation Little Vittles in 1948 and 1949.

Once in Berlin, as residents toured the exhibits aboard the *Spirit of Freedom*, Halvorsen received yet another reminder of the ties that bind him to the children of fifty years earlier. A man approached him and held out an old handkerchief with the German words "'Little Vit-tles' for the children of Lt. Halvorsen. Please return this parachute to a Military Policeman at Tempelhof Airport." "Please forgive me," the fellow said. "I just couldn't part with my parachute, my personal symbol of freedom."

The next year found Halvorsen heading back to Eastern Europe, where violence had erupted once again in Serbia, in the province of Kosovo. The Air Force invited him to fly on a C-130 making a supply run to a Kosovar refugee camp in Albania. With supplies of candy and

Halvorsen with Kosovar refugee children at Camp Hope in Albania. (1999)

gum—along with a large collection of donated stuffed animals and school supplies—he reported for duty. This time he was able to deliver his treats in person, flying into the refugee camp in a helicopter. "What a reception," he recalls. "These children had the same bright faces, appreciation, and optimism exhibited by the Berlin kids at the barbed wire fence in 1948. . . . They had hope because of people in America who . . . knew they were in trouble and promised to stand by them. Hope is still the name of the game."

Hope was what Halvorsen's Christmas drops to the people of the Micronesian Islands were all about. In 2000 and 2002 Gail joined a flight crew parachuting Christmas boxes onto seven remote islands. The containers were filled with Christmas treats, toys, and other surprises for the children—as well as much needed supplies, such as machetes, fishing gear, and clothing.

In his late-eighties Gail Halvorsen is still qualified to fly C-54s, and he can be seen from time to time copiloting the *Spirit of Freedom* to air shows and celebrations. He also flies his own single-engine plane around Utah and its neighboring states.

Halvorsen still makes the occasional candy drop over schools, and he continues to be honored in one fashion or another for his legacy. In 1999 he was inducted into the Air Tanker Association Hall of Fame. In 2001 the military named its new twenty-five-thousand-pound (eleven-thousand-kilogram) aircraft loader the Halvorsen Loader. And on October 10, 2005, Gail Halvorsen attended, as an honored guest, closure ceremonies at Rhein-Main Air Force Base. "Rhein-Main has been a pretty big part of my life," he said, as the United States turned the base back over to Germany. Later that month Halvorsen was involved in candy drops to Mississippi children living with the terrible destruction of Hurricane Katrina. He noted that the homes in south Mississippi looked familiar. "You can look right through the buildings. . . . It was the same way in Berlin."

In 2008 Gail Halvorsen returned to Germany to commemorate the sixtieth anniversary of the Berlin Airlift. Though he was eighty-seven, his schedule of appearances around the country and the globe had not diminished, and neither had his enthusiasm for keeping alive the spirit of Operation Vittles and Operation Little Vittles. If you were to ask how he feels about the honors and opportunities that have come over the years as a result of his candy drops, Halvorsen would likely shake his head and give his standard, unassuming answer: "All this for two sticks of gum!"

Historical Note

Adolf Hitler launched World War II by attacking Poland in September of 1939. In the early days of a war that lasted six years, Hitler and the leaders of his ruling political party, the Nazis, made an alliance with Russia, known at that time as the Soviet Union (USSR). But the Nazis and Soviets had never liked one another, so the alliance was shaky at best. As it turned out, Hitler had never planned to keep his agreement with the Soviet Union, and on June 22, 1941, the German armies attacked Russia.

The Soviets were forced to change their allegiances in order to survive the rapid onslaught of Hitler's blitzkrieg (lightning war).

The Brandenburg Gate, one of Berlin's most recognized landmarks, was damaged by Russian artillery.

The Allies—a coalition of several countries, including Great Britain and the United States—also needed help against Germany, so they agreed to join forces with the Russians. The Soviets were finally able to drive back the Nazis, but the German armies exacted a terrible toll on the Russian people, twenty million of whom died during the war.

By the end of 1944 the tide of conflict in Europe clearly had changed. The Allies were driving German forces out of occupied countries and back behind the borders of their own land. The Soviets attacked Germany from the east, the other Allies from the west.

The Allied powers decided that the Soviets would be the ones to take Berlin, Germany's capital city. Seeking revenge for the twenty million Russian war deaths, the Soviet army was merciless as it marched through Germany. Berlin, the symbol of Nazi power, paid a heavy price. Already bombed into crumbling piles of rubble by the United States and Britain, Berlin soon surrendered to the Soviets. Hitler, refusing to be taken alive, shot himself.

The Western Allies had already fought and beaten Germany once before—in World War I (1914–1918). From that experience they learned that further punishing a conquered people creates resentment. The crushing war debt they placed on Germany after the first World War not only added to the people's pain but also destroyed their pride. Soon the country began hoping for a national "savior"—someone to restore Germany to its former glory. The "savior" who surfaced, Adolf Hitler, was instead a destroying angel for both Germany and the Allies.

The United States, in particular, did not want to make the same mistake again and proposed the Marshall Plan, a program to rebuild a free and prosperous Germany. The Soviets protested this policy, and the Western Allies soon realized there was little hope for Russian co-operation. Before the United States, Britain, and France arrived to take control of their respective sectors of Berlin, the Soviets disman-tled and removed from those areas such facilities as power stations, factories, and telephone-switching stations. They hoped to keep their former friends from meddling in their affairs by forcing them to abandon Berlin.

As tensions grew, the Russians decided a blockade of the city would at last force the Western Allies to leave. The Berlin Airlift was the surprising answer to a plan they thought foolproof. The Soviets made some attempts to stop the Airlift by practicing anti-aircraft fire near the air corridors into Berlin and by "buzzing" American cargo planes—flying past at top speed and narrowly missing them. They even bribed West Berliners by offering fresh vegetables, coal, and other necessities to those who agreed to sign up for East Berlin ration cards. Very few West Berliners—perhaps four percent—participated in the Soviets' ploy to win them over.

In the end the Berlin Airlift proved successful, but the United States and Soviet Union's mistrust and fear of one another had already engendered the Cold War—a period of tension that began with the Berlin blockade and continued with the threat of nuclear conflict. Much of the world was alarmed by the Soviets' iron-fisted rule of Eastern Europe. Countries behind the USSR's "Iron Curtain" became so isolated from the rest of the planet that little was known about what was happening within their borders. In 1961 the Soviet Union built a concrete and barbed-wire wall to separate East and West Berlin. Guards with machine guns manned the towers and stopped any who tried to cross.

The burned-out shell of the Reichstag sits at the center of what is left of Berlin.

It took four decades before things in the Soviet Union changed. In 1989, as a more liberal brand of leadership took hold in Russia, the Berlin Wall came down, and Soviet control of Eastern Europe ended. Today Germany is once again a unified country, and East and West Berlin have come together as a single city.

Gail Halvorsen looks out over his land in a Rocky Mountain valley in Utah.

Author's Note

I had long been familiar with the Berlin Airlift, or "Operation Vittles," which I had learned about in school. However, I knew nothing about "Operation Little Vittles" until a dignified older gentleman dressed in an Air Force uniform came to speak to the youth group at our church. This was my introduction to Gail Halvorsen, the Berlin Candy Bomber. His story captivated me that day and eventually led me to write this book. But first I spent months mulling over what retired Colonel Halvorsen had said. Finally I decided to write a picture book about his amazing candy drops. I completed the manuscript only to discover that Margot Theis Raven had beaten me to the punch. *Mercedes and the Chocolate Pilot* (Sleeping Bear Press, 2002) had just hit the bookstore shelves.

I dumped my plans for a picture book about Halvorsen. Instead, I realized I'd really rather write a longer book, one with photographs documenting the Candy Bomber's exploits. I soon discovered that Halvorsen had written his own book for adults about his experiences during the Berlin Airlift (*The Berlin Candy Bomber*, Horizon, 2002). It was replete with photographs and other images, many of which would be perfect for the book I envisioned.

I found a phone number for the Halvorsen residence in a nearby Utah town and gave it a try. Gail's cordial voice greeted me on the other end of the line. The Halvorsens live in Utah during the warm months and in Arizona the rest of the time, so I was fortunate to have called during the right part of the year. I introduced myself and explained what I hoped to do with his story. To my delight, Gail invited me to come by the house to talk further about my plans. A week later I found myself chatting with him in his living room and looking at his photograph collection.

The most rewarding aspect of writing this book was getting to know Gail Halvorsen. He helped me every step of the way to make this project a success. He allowed me to carry home an enormous box filled with pictures, newspaper clippings, letters and drawings from German children, and more—the very sorts of images you see within these pages. I scanned well over three hundred items and placed the images on a compact disc for Gail. He was ecstatic to have his memories digitized—so much so that he guarded them for my use. I couldn't believe it when I received a call from Gail asking if someone else could use a few photos from the CD. Of course, I told Gail that they were his to give, not mine, but I was impressed and humbled by the respect he afforded me. That is simply the kind of person

The author stands with Gail Halvorsen, the Wasatch Mountains in the background. (June 25, 2009)

Gail Halvorsen is. It is not difficult to understand why, after sixty years, so many people in Germany and around the world hold him in such high esteem.

I began this project because I wanted to share a compelling and important story with a young audience. I ended the endeavor thankful for the privilege and honor it provided me. I discovered in Gail Halvorsen and the other men of "Operation Little Vittles" true American heroes—heroes as much for their compassion as for their bravery and moral strength. Their example has uplifted me, and I hope that my recounting of their exploits will do the same for my readers.

Selected References

All quotations come from the author's personal interviews with Gail Halvorsen or from the references listed below.

Center for Balkan Development.
   http://www.friendsofbosnia.org/edu_bos.html
Cherny, Andrei. *The Candy Bombers: The Untold Story of the Berlin Airlift and America's Finest Hour.* New York: Putnam, 2008.
Halvorsen, Gail S. Speech to National Geographic Society (tape recording). Washington, DC, February 18, 1949.
Halvorsen, Gail S. *The Berlin Candy Bomber.* 3rd ed. Bountiful, UT: Horizon, 2002.
Huschke, Wolfgang J. *The Candy Bombers: The Berlin Airlift 1948/49.* Berlin: Metropol, 1999.

Irvin, David W. *Highway to Freedom.* Paducah, KY: Turner Publishing, 2002.

Launius, Roger D., and John W. Leland. Military Airlift Command Oral History Program, Interview No. 1: Colonel Gail S. Halvorsen, USAF-Retired, May 13, 1988. Scott Air Force Base, IL: November 1988.

Pennacchio, Charles F. "The East German Communists and the Origins of the Berlin Blockade Crisis." *East European Quarterly* 29, no. 3 (Fall 1995): 293–314.

Shirer, William L. *The Rise and Fall of the Third Reich: A History of Nazi Germany.* New York: Simon & Schuster, 1950.

Symposium: Final Status for Kosovo: Untying the Gordian Knot. http://pbosnia.kentlaw.edu/symposium/the-map-final-copy-with-proof-corr.doc

For Further Reading

Ayer, Eleanor H. *Berlin.* Cities at War. Toronto: New Discovery/ Maxwell Macmillan, 1992.

Raven, Margot Theis. *Mercedes and the Chocolate Pilot.* Chelsea, MI: Sleeping Bear Press, 2002.

Westerfield, Scott. *The Berlin Airlift.* Turning Points in American History. Manitowoc, WI: Silver Burdett, 1989.